2006

Sylvia

You are alway[s] in our hearts. ! So precious to us. May this book encoura- you as you have been a blessing to us.

Love Keth Carla & Beth

xoxo

D0341179

YOUR LOVE
is AMAZING

A 30-DAY WORSHIP ADVENTURE

INTEGRITY'S
i WORSH!P
A TOTAL WORSHIP EXPERIENCE

presents

YOUR LOVE
is AMAZING

A 30-DAY WORSHIP ADVENTURE

ROBERTA CROTEAU

INTEGRITY®
PUBLISHERS
Nashville

Your Love Is Amazing

Devotions copyright © 2003 by Roberta Croteau.

Published by Integrity Publishers, a division of Integrity Media, Inc.,
5250 Virginia Way, Suite 110, Brentwood, TN 37027.

HELPING PEOPLE WORLDWIDE EXPERIENCE *the* MANIFEST PRESENCE *of* GOD.

Scripture quotations used in this book are from The Holy Bible, New
International Version (NIV). ©1973, 1978, 1984, International Bible Society.
Used by permission of Zondervan Bible Publishers.

Cover and Interior Design: The Office of Bill Chiaravalle / www.officeofbc.com

ISBN 1-59145-082-9

Printed in the United States of America
03 04 05 06 07 RRD 9 8 7 6 5 4 3 2

TABLE OF CONTENTS

L O V E

"Someday, after mastering the winds, the waves, the tides and gravity, we shall harness for God the energies of love, and then, for a second time in the history of the world, man will have discovered fire."

Pierre Teilhard de Chardin

JESUS LOVER OF MY SOUL
John Ezzy, Daniel Grul & Steve McPherson

Jesus lover of my soul
Jesus I will never let You go
You've taken me from the miry clay
You've set my feet upon the rock
And now I know

I love You, I need You
Though my world may fall
I'll never let You go
My Savior, my closest Friend
I will worship You until the very end

When Paul wrote about the three great things remaining —faith, hope, and love—he wasn't kidding about the greatest of these being love. Love is the thread that runs through the entire story of God's attachment to His people. He has written His name on our hearts and refuses to take no for an answer.

Pascal said, "The heart has its reasons that reason knows nothing of." God is the best proof of that. His heart is consumed, not by logic, nor reason, nor rules, but by passion. When it comes to love, He's ready to do anything in the name of it. The first Christmas morning was only the beginning of the incredible lengths He was willing to go. And if God truly is love, Jesus was the walking, breathing, in-our-faces proof. He started a party two thousand years ago and still hasn't stopped inviting everyone to come.

He was love, is love, and oozes love. Love tinges His every decision, His every move. He dined and danced with the rebels and losers and didn't care what the neighbors thought. When everyone wanted to stone the woman caught in her guilt, Jesus dropped the stones and let love speak the verdict.

GOD'S HEART IS CONSUMED,
NOT BY LOGIC, NOR REASON,
NOR RULES, BUT BY PASSION.
WHEN IT COMES TO LOVE,
HE'S READY TO DO ANYTHING
IN THE NAME OF IT.

Opening His door to any sorry fool who knocked, He was the only one who took in any story they wanted to tell. It didn't matter. Like He said, the sick didn't need a doctor, and He didn't come to let the saints feel even better about themselves.

One

He came looking for the lost, broken sinners who never even knew they had gold-engraved invitations to the party, let alone the right to RSVP. All we needed was love and He knew it. Of course He knew it. It was His plan all along.

While all the party poopers stood outside and watched through the windows, shouting their lists of all the rules He was breaking, He partied on. They really thought He needed to

HE CAME LOOKING FOR THE LOST, BROKEN SINNERS WHO NEVER EVEN KNEW THEY HAD GOLD-ENGRAVED INVITATIONS.

learn. They really thought He didn't know. They actually

assumed He was breaking God's laws when He was the one who carved them in stone in the first place.

He knew the rules. He knew the laws. And He also knew—actually, He made it so—that the greatest law of all was love.

In the end Love conquers all. Love even trumps justice. Amazing grace, they call it, and it's a grace He's extended to all His creation every day since the world first began. It's a stupendous, magnificent, beautiful thing—this thing called God's love. And it is, indeed, amazing.

If love truly is the greatest gift of all, how are you sharing it in your own life, with God and with those around you?

RECEIVE

"Be joyful always; pray continually;
give thanks in all circumstances..."

I Thessalonians 5:16-18

LORD HAVE MERCY
Steve Merkel

Jesus I've forgotten
The words that You have spoken
Promises that burned within my heart
Have now grown dim
With a doubting heart I follow
The paths of earthly wisdom
Forgive me for my unbelief
Renew the fire again

Lord have mercy
Christ have mercy
Lord have mercy on me

In the hit TV show *Trading Spaces,* friendly neighbors give a lackluster room in their homes over to each other and a couple of opinionated designers, and trust them to deliver a totally new look to it. They're hoping that somehow, miraculously, the designer assigned to their home will have the same taste they do. In the most captivating episodes, that usually isn't the case.

The intriguing part is watching the shocked couple with the new, not-to-their-liking room trying to graciously thank their neighbor friends, the designers, and the show host for something you know is coming down as soon as the production truck pulls away. It's hard to cultivate a grateful response when disappointment is clouding the way. Most of the time, as someone watching from afar, you have to say, "Well, it's better than what you had before—give it a chance."

EVERYONE WAS SITTING
AROUND WAITING FOR A
WARRIOR MESSIAH—SOMEONE
WITH A ROOM WITH A VIEW
OF A PROMISED LAND.

When Jesus traded His own space in Heaven for the
chance to make something new of the dying old world before
Him, it was hard to find even one grateful party. Everyone was
sitting around waiting for a warrior Messiah—someone with a
room with a view of a promised land. They expected Him to
arrive and, in one broad stroke, vanquish their enemies and
make everything right again.

Instead they got a Prince of Peace, who to be sure was
ready to do some rearranging. Trouble was, He was more

interested in their hearts than their land. And apparently the only enemy He was interested in vanquishing was the unbelievable baggage of expectations and demands everyone seemed to be carrying around with them—both for Him and for their own lives. What no one expected was that all the change He left behind would be so beautiful. By the time they discovered it, He wasn't around to thank—in person anyway.

> APPARENTLY THE ONLY ENEMY HE
> WAS INTERESTED IN VANQUISHING
> WAS THE UNBELIEVABLE BAGGAGE
> OF EXPECTATIONS AND DEMANDS
> EVERYONE SEEMED TO BE CARRYING
> AROUND WITH THEM.

As Joni Mitchell sang, "Don't it always seem to go, that you don't know what you've got 'til it's gone."

Sometimes the best gifts come in unexpected packages. If you're willing to be patient and wait to discover what

IF YOU'RE WILLING TO BE
PATIENT, YOU MAY FIND THAT
EVERY DAY, EVERY MOMENT,
EVERY PERSON YOU MEET IS A
GIFT TO YOUR LIFE.

might not be obvious at first, you may find that every day, every moment, every person you meet is a gift to your life. And they all come from the ultimate Giver of good things.

It truly is better to give than to receive, but a grateful receiver can be a gift back to the giver. Think of the gifts God has given you and your response to those gifts. Cultivate your own grateful heart.

DARE

"I will heal their waywardness and love them freely..."

Hosea 14:4

COME THOU FOUNT
Robert Robinson

Come Thou Fount of ev'ry blessing
Tune my heart to sing Thy grace
Streams of mercy never ceasing
Call for songs of loudest praise

O to grace how great a debtor
Daily I'm constrained to be
Let Thy grace, Lord, like a fetter
Bind my wand'ring heart to Thee

Prone to wander, Lord, I feel it
Prone to leave the God I love
Here's my heart, Lord, take and seal it
Seal it for Thy courts above

Three

When God asked His prophet Hosea to marry the local loose woman, the groom must have thought someone was off His rocker. Spend your lifetime convincing the world you are the messenger of God's words of morality, justice, and truth—and then He asks you to . . . what?! It's probably, at its core, one of the funniest stories in the Bible. Leave it to God to drive someone crazy to help make a point. Not to mention imagining this whole story from Gomer's point of view: One day you're the scourge of the town, and the next day you're walking down the aisle with the village preacherman.

Makes you wonder if anyone knew what was going on that day. But something amazing usually does happen when you let go and let God do whatever He wants.

So Gomer marries Hosea, and they have a few children

with depressing names, and life sort of goes on for the odd couple. Until Gomer's old life beckons and that age-old temptation returns. Perhaps she couldn't really believe she could be loved. Or that she was worth being loved. Or maybe she believed she wasn't good enough to live like someone who was loved.

Whatever her reasons, she strayed. And Hosea came home, but instead of kicking her back to the streets, he just said over and over again, "How can I ever leave you? How could I ever not love you?" Hosea's heart may have been crushed by her betrayal, but his love was indestructible. God, it seems, must have looked down and said, "See, do you get it yet? Anyone? This is what I've been saying all along."

You can almost imagine Him chuckle when He first dreams up the absurd plot. If You can prove to one of Your creations that the love they have for another person is a mere sliver of the love You have for them, maybe—just maybe—they'd start to understand. That boundless, fathomless ocean that is God's love seems limited only by our inability to accept it. It's just too wild for words.

> IF YOU CAN PROVE TO ONE OF
> YOUR CREATIONS THAT THE LOVE
> THEY HAVE FOR ANOTHER
> PERSON IS A MERE SLIVER OF THE
> LOVE YOU HAVE FOR THEM,
> MAYBE—JUST MAYBE—THEY'D
> START TO UNDERSTAND.

Charlie Chaplin, the old-time actor and film director, was no stranger to absurdities himself when he declared, "Life is a tragedy when seen in close-up, but a comedy in long-shot." Almost everything's funny when you're not in the middle of it. So the farther you walk away from something that breaks your heart, the closer you come to realizing that you are surrounded by a love so unreal, it would take a miracle to make you believe it.

Hosea got a close-up view—in fact, he got the leading role in God's attempt to show the world His love. No matter how far you go, the script reads, there is absolutely nothing you can do to shake Him. Many have tried, including Gomer—who put in one of history's strongest performances—but so far no one has succeeded.

Have you ever tried to run away from love? It is when we are most unsure of ourselves that we doubt the love of others. What are ways you can remind yourself of God's constant love and presence in your life?

_____

_____

_____

_____

_____

_____

_____

_____

_____

_____

_____

_____

_____

_____

_____

_____

_____

_____

_____

REJOICE

*"...Though the olive crop fails and the fields produce
no food, though there are no sheep in the pen and
no cattle in the stalls, yet I will rejoice in the LORD,
I will be joyful in God my Savior."*

Habakkuk 3:17, 18

GOD WILL MAKE A WAY
Don Moen

*God will make a way
Where there seems to be no way
He works in ways we cannot see
He will make a way for me
He will be my guide
Hold me closely to His side
With love and strength
For each new day
He will make a way
He will make a way*

*By a roadway in the wilderness
He'll lead me
And rivers in the desert will I see
Heaven and earth will fade
But His Word will still remain
He will do something new today*

Four

All of us face unexpected challenges as we go through our lives. Things don't always turn out the way we expected them to. Darkness falls, clouds gather, and shadows come, but our faith and confidence in God need never be shaken. And when we face difficult times and trials, He will be with us to make a way where there seems to be no way.

Have you ever felt that God was a million miles away and wasn't even listening to the cry of your heart? Have you ever poured out your heart to God, desperate for an answer but the answer didn't come? I think all of us have experienced this at some point in our lives. Does it mean that God has forgotten us? Does His silence mean that He doesn't care? No. The Bible tells us that He will never leave us or forsake us (Hebrews 13:5) and that God is able to do exceedingly abundantly above all that we could ever ask or think (Ephesians 3:20)! Our solutions to our problems are limited to what we can ask or think. But God's solutions are *above* all that we could ever ask or think. Isaiah tells us that His thoughts and His ways are far above ours (55:8-9).

So what do we do when we are going through a difficult time? Habakkuk 3:18 says, "Yet I will rejoice in the LORD, I will be joyful in God my Savior." We are supposed to exult, to find great joy in the Lord and rejoice in our God who is our salvation! Why? Because everything is perfect in our lives? Not necessarily. I heard someone say once that we don't have to deny the reality of our situation, whether it's physical, financial, spiritual, or emotional; we just don't have to accept it as the finality. In other words, we need to see our situation through the eyes of faith. Remember, God has the final word. Circumstances may be telling you that you are finished and you have run out of options. But God has promised in His

Word that He will make a roadway in the wilderness and a river in the desert (Isaiah 43:19). When we have exhausted our own resources, God is about to show us that He is not limited to our ideas and solutions.

> WE DON'T HAVE TO DENY THE
> REALITY OF OUR SITUATION,
> WHETHER IT'S PHYSICAL,
> FINANCIAL, SPIRITUAL,
> OR EMOTIONAL. WE JUST
> DON'T HAVE TO ACCEPT IT
> AS THE FINALITY.

Luke 1:37 tells us that "nothing will be impossible with God." So if you are going through a difficult situation right now, don't allow the enemy to come into your life and steal your song. Make a choice to bless the Lord. Make a choice to exalt Him, even in the midst of a difficult circumstance, because God is working in ways you cannot see! So let's lift our voices and worship Him. Let's lift our voices and sing to Him and praise Him with all our heart because He is an awesome God and worthy to be praised. And remember, sometimes the most intense praise comes in the midst of the most intense pain.

What difficult situations has God brought you through? And who and what did He use to do it? How were you able to bless the Lord even in the midst of your pain?

_____

_____

_____

_____

_____

_____

_____

_____

_____

_____

_____

_____

_____

_____

_____

_____

_____

_____

WONDER

"Beauty will save the world."

Fyodor Dostoevsky

POWER OF YOUR LOVE
Geoff Bullock

Lord I come to You
Let my heart be changed renewed
Flowing from the grace
That I've found in You
And Lord I've come to know
The weaknesses I see in me
Will be stripped away
By the power of Your love

Hold me close
And let Your love surround me
Bring me near
And draw me to Your side
And as I wait
I'll rise up like the eagle
And I will soar with You
Your Spirit leads me on
By the power of Your love

Beauty is in the eye of the beholder, or so they say. But sometimes the most beautiful things in the world can't even be seen.

With all the splendor that surrounds creation, it's mesmerizing to think that what we see is barely scratching the surface. For beauty is, in fact, way more than skin deep. God, the Master Designer, uses the seen and the unseen to dazzle us from afar and to plant His beautiful works both without and within. Simone Weil wrote, "The soul's natural inclination to love beauty is the trap God most frequently uses in order to win it and open it to the breath from on high."

God is not only the Creator of all things beautiful, but also Giver of the gift that enables us to recognize beauty. His trap is a circle of love—enticing, beguiling, and enchanting. As the poet wrote, "Love drew the circle that took us in." God

takes us in for our own good and sets before us all the glories

> GOD TAKES US IN FOR OUR
>
> OWN GOOD AND SETS BEFORE
>
> US ALL THE GLORIES OF
>
> HEAVEN AND EARTH.

of Heaven and earth. Jesus declared that "eye had not seen and

ear had not heard" the amazing things God has in store for

those who love Him. If not even Solomon in all his splendor

could match the glory of the swaying lilies of the field, how

much more must be the splendor God has for those with eyes

to see? Just imagine what could be waiting while you breathe

deep and take in what's here right now.

When the Bible declares that the mountains will sing and the rocks will cry out the message of God's love, it's merely another picture of the length, the height, the breadth, and the depth that God will go to lure us out of our suffocating shells and awake us to the wonder of what He has made. He prom-

JUST IMAGINE WHAT COULD
BE WAITING WHILE YOU
BREATHE DEEP AND TAKE IN
WHAT'S HERE RIGHT NOW.

ises beauty even from the ashes. Ecclesiastes assures us that "he has made everything beautiful in his time," and that "he has also set eternity in the hearts of men; yet they cannot fathom what God has done from beginning to end" (3:11).

Heaven truly is found in every grain of sand and every wildflower, because God's love and His hands have made every one of them. If He can't make us see it with the obvious, He'll set it before us with the miraculous.

It really is a beautiful sight.

How has God trapped you in His love?
What can you do to draw others into that circle?

_____

_____

_____

_____

_____

_____

_____

_____

_____

_____

_____

_____

_____

_____

_____

_____

_____

_____

HONOR

"Be true to your work, your word, and your friend."

Henry David Thoreau

ROCK OF AGES
Rita Baloche

There is no Rock
There is no God like our God
No other name
Worthy of all our praise
The Rock of Salvation
That cannot be moved
He's proven himself
To be faithful and true
There is no Rock
There is no God like ours

Rock of Ages
Jesus is the Rock
Rock of Ages
Jesus is the Rock
Rock of Ages
Jesus is the Rock
There is no Rock
There is no God like ours

Six

In the movie *To Kill a Mockingbird,* Gregory Peck patiently tried to explain to his daughter, Scout, why people hate. She'd already seen it all around her: a strange boy who had condemned himself to a hermit's life for not being the same as everyone else, and the poor boy at school whose only crime

"DO TO OTHERS AS YOU
WOULD HAVE THEM DO TO YOU."
IT WAS AS SIMPLE—AND AS
COMPLICATED—AS THAT.

seemed to be being poor. Then, looming over all of them, the innocent man already hung for nothing more than being someone no one else wanted around. Someone they feared because they could not understand—and hate became the easiest way out.

Somehow in his gentle explanation, Peck's character managed to sum up life's pursuits in much the same way that Jesus did two thousand years earlier: "Do to others as you would have them do to you." It was as simple—and as complicated—as that. Even we who are not children listening on someone's knee know that it's much easier said than done. But when all is said and done, it really is the truth of life, the embodiment of what Micah says when he declares what God requires of us: "to act justly and to love mercy and to walk humbly with your God" (6:8).

Who can forget that incredible courtroom scene—a place where hate collided with the truth and Atticus Finch was in the fight of his life? As a simple lawyer, he knew the not-so-simple truth. When it would have been easier to walk away, easier to let hate take over all reason and go back home—away from all these unreasonable souls consumed by their own prejudices—he did the right thing. He stayed and he fought for a friend. He fought for innocence lost and for the innocence

> WHEN IT WOULD HAVE BEEN
> EASIER TO WALK AWAY, EASIER
> TO LET HATE TAKE OVER ALL
> REASON AND GO BACK HOME,
> HE DID THE RIGHT THING.

found again. Maybe deep down he knew that what he helped others find in themselves meant that he, too, could keep it alive in himself.

There are no easy answers. And even in the movies, there isn't always a happy ending. Being true to his word, Atticus found, didn't guarantee happiness. It didn't even guarantee fairness. Yet it was still a lesson worth teaching his daughter, his neighbors, his enemies, and his friends. He said it was a sin to kill a mockingbird because mockingbirds just go busily about their lives and do nothing to hurt us. God gives the same warning when it comes to people. Let go of the hurt and the "eyes for eyes." . . . Love is all you need after all. And love can cover a multitude of sins.

Sometimes doing the right thing is the hardest thing. Write about a time in your life in which you made that honorable choice.

_____

_____

_____

_____

_____

_____

_____

_____

_____

_____

_____

_____

_____

_____

_____

_____

_____

SHINE

"One could not pluck a flower, without troubling a star."

Loren Eiseley

HERE I AM TO WORSHIP
Tim Hughes

Light of the world
You stepped down into darkness
Opened my eyes, let me see
Beauty that made
This heart adore You
Hope of a life spent with You

So here I am to worship
Here I am to bow down
Here I am to say that You're my God
And You're altogether lovely
Altogether worthy
Altogether wonderful to me

King of all days
Oh so highly exalted
Glorious in heaven above
Humbly You came
To the earth You created
All for love's sake became poor

An old Serbian proverb advises, "Be humble, for you are made of earth. Be noble, for you are made of stars." It doesn't take much to accept the first part—but believing the second phrase is the challenge. Could it ever be true that we contain even just a sprinkle of the sparkle of Heaven?

Jesus was a bundle of contradictions, so it's not that surprising that anyone trying to follow Him ends up caught in the web of His paradoxes. We are at once led to believe we are mere

WE ARE AT ONCE LED TO
BELIEVE WE ARE MERE DIRT
AND SPIT BROUGHT TO LIFE,
AND IN THE VERY NEXT BREATH
WE ARE THE IMAGE OF GOD.

dirt and spit brought to life, and in the very next breath we are the image of God, encompassing every ounce of His glory and beauty. Sometimes it's hard to figure out where the balance is. Am I too worthless to go on or too worthwhile to give up? I believe Jesus showed up just to prove the latter.

He even played the game Himself for a while. As Philippians says, He was the one "who, being in very nature God, did not consider equality with God something to be grasped, but made himself nothing . . . being made in human

THE MAKER OF THE STARS
STEPPED DOWN TO EARTH TO
SHOW US WHAT WE'RE MADE OF.

likeness" (2:6-7). The Maker of the stars stepped down to earth to show us what we're made of: a touch of Heaven and a whole lot of earth. He was willing to stoop to our level to show us the heights we could attain.

Maybe it isn't such a contradiction after all. God molded an Adam from the dust of the ground—the earth He had already poured His love into—and then in one divine kiss,

WE HAVE FEET OF CLAY AND A

SOUL MADE TO SOAR THE SKIES.

breathed the life of Heaven into his soul. We are as much a creation of what is above as we are of what is beneath us. We have feet of clay and a soul made to soar the skies.

A quirky old country song lamented, "It's hard to be humble when you're perfect in every way." Good for a laugh, but luckily, we're daily given reminders of just how far we have to go so that we may resist really ever believing we are that wonderful. At the same time, God lets us keep our starry-eyed hearts set on Him and the promise of what can be. We remain children of the living God—a noble people with a marvelous inheritance waiting, even while plodding the dusty roads before us.

Humanity and divinity mingled was the gift of Jesus to the world. How can you manifest that combination in your own life to the glory of God?

_____

_____

_____

_____

_____

_____

_____

_____

_____

_____

_____

_____

_____

_____

_____

_____

_____

_____

DREAM

"Dum spiro, spero." *("While I breathe, I hope.")*

I WILL CELEBRATE
Rita Baloche

I will celebrate
Sing unto the Lord
Sing to the Lord a new song
I will celebrate
Sing unto the Lord
Sing to the Lord a new song

With my heart rejoicing within
With my mind focused on Him
With my hands raised to the heavens
All I am worshiping Him

Eight

It has been said that what we truly want in life is found, not at the destination, but in what we experience on the journey there. For many, many years though, I dreamed of visiting Paris. That destination was the ultimate goal. In my mind's eye,

> WHAT WE TRULY WANT IN LIFE IS
> FOUND, NOT AT THE DESTINATION,
> BUT IN WHAT WE EXPERIENCE
> ON THE JOURNEY THERE.

it was going to be a glorious feast for my eyes, my ears, and of course, my palate. Paris is, the magazines proclaim, a gastronomical extravaganza. So it seemed like the universe was truly unfolding as it should as I boarded a plane to France to live out my dream. With six friends, eyes aglitter, we set off with a mere but promising twenty-four hours before us to discover the City of Lights.

The limited time was no problem; my Paris dream was still intact. Here's how I imagined it: Arrive in Paris. Stroll the boulevards. Reminisce about all the historical things that happened on each spot as we walked the streets. Then, perhaps after a whimsical mime performed for us, we'd saunter over to

THIS WAS GOING TO BE THE
MEMORY OF A LIFETIME.

Notre Dame, have a grand moment of spiritual enlightenment, cross the bridge and touch the books Hemingway and Stein and Fitzgerald pored over in the quaint coffee and book shops along the River Seine . . . and then, the *coup d'grace* . . . the Eiffel Tower. We'd gasp at the beauty of the city from on high and then we'd dine on unbelievable French fare in the Jules Verne restaurant nestled within its grand steel structure. I even brought *the* dress. This was going to be the memory of a lifetime.

Here's what really happened: We arrived late. Some of us were grumpy. (It was only noon; I wasn't in that group . . . yet.) My dream still buoyed my soul. Three years of high school French between the lot of us left us completely unable to figure out where we were and how to get anywhere. We wandered streets. We were lost, hadn't officially "seen" anything yet, and time was ticking away. And then, my raggle of friends decided they were hungry. *This is good,* I think . . . *This way we'll really appreciate our Eiffel Tower dinner tonight.* No dice. Ahead of us my friends spotted—and I am not making this up—"Happy Burger" (it didn't even have the sense to call itself "*Le Burg de Joie.*") And they went in! And they ate! Happy Burgers and fries! This was not my idea of Parisian cuisine. My dream was getting more than a little ragged around the edges. Surely making one's dreams come true shouldn't be this frustrating? . . .

But there's more to this story. See tomorrow.

*Remember a time when everything went wrong
in your life, only to later to discover that it
was the path toward something very right.*

_____

_____

_____

_____

_____

_____

_____

_____

_____

_____

_____

_____

_____

_____

_____

_____

_____

_____

H O P E

"Trust in the LORD with all your heart and lean not on your own understanding; in all your ways acknowledge him and he will make your paths straight."

Proverbs 3:5-6

MEET WITH ME
Lamont Heibert

I'm here to meet with You
Come and meet with me
I'm here to find You
Reveal Yourself to me

As I wait
You make me strong
As I long
You draw me to Your arms
As I stand
And sing Your praise
You come, You come
And You fill this place
Won't You come

The pursuit of the dream continued . . . We found Notre Dame and raced through. I was awe-inspired, but only had a few seconds to gasp. The group reluctantly went "off course" for me (from what "grand plan," I still don't know) to do a quick browse through the Shakespeare and Company Bookstore. There was no time to buy a book. Off to the subway and then the Eiffel Tower. *Okay, at least there is still that,* I thought. Of course, there was no time to change into our finery. We'd be doing this whole jaunt in jeans. We got to the tower and into the lines. "Um," my friends boldly tried to break the obvious news, "we're in jeans, so guess we can't eat in the fancy restaurant. But we'll find an authentic French café when we're done and it will almost be the same."

Let's just fast-forward here to say, we went up; we took in the view; we lost one of our group. (Do not ask how you lose someone IN the tower—just trust me, it's doable.) She was missing for three hours. (See previous parenthetical statement). By the time we all found each other, it was too late to go anywhere. We got to the hotel. One of our group ran to the Paris McDonald's, and we finished our evening in "Paree" with take-out Big Macs and I guess the most "French" French fries one can have.

WE DID NOTHING THE WAY
I HAD WANTED OR PLANNED,
AND YET REMARKABLY, MY
TRIP TO PARIS REMAINS ONE
OF THE FONDEST HIGHLIGHTS
OF MY TRAVELING LIFE.

Nine

That was how it actually happened. We did nothing the way I had wanted or planned, and yet remarkably, my trip to Paris remains one of the fondest highlights of my traveling life. I never dined on French gourmet, but the memories of what

> WHEN YOU LOOK AT THE POST-
> CARDS FROM YOUR JOURNEY, I'LL
> BET YOU END UP SMILING AT THE
> MEMORIES MORE THAN YOU END
> UP CRINGING AT THE MISSTEPS.

happened instead are absolutely delicious. The laughter from the string of mishaps has echoed through the time that has passed—and as for regrets, I have not a single one. Given the chance to do it all again, I wouldn't change a single minute of that ill-fated trip.

Being given the chance to live our lives over again might seem tempting at first, but when you stop to take a look at the postcards from your journey, I'll bet you end up smiling at the memories many more times than you end up cringing at the missteps. And in the end, it truly is the journey and not the destination. It's the dream and not just the coming true. It's who we are now and not just who we'll become. *C'est la vie.* Live it.

On life's journey we have many ups and downs.
What is the best thing so far that has happened on yours?
What is the worst?

_____

_____

_____

_____

_____

_____

_____

_____

_____

_____

_____

_____

_____

_____

_____

_____

LISTEN

*"Be still, and know that I am God; I will be
exalted among the nations, I will be exalted in the earth."*

Psalm 46:10

THE POTTER'S HAND
Darlene Zschech

*Beautiful Lord
Wonderful Savior
I know for sure all of my days
Are held in Your hand
Crafted into Your perfect plan
You gently call me
Into Your presence
Guiding me by Your Holy Spirit
Teach me dear Lord
To live all of my life
Through Your eyes
I'm captured by Your holy calling
Set me apart
I know You're drawing me to Yourself
Lead me Lord I pray*

Growing up in the church, I have noticed something the Body of Christ does quite well: Talk! We talk all the time! Sometimes we talk too much! No matter where you go to church, there is always somebody with something to say. And if we're not talking, we're singing. I think it is safe to say that the church spends most of its time making some kind of noise.

Now don't get me wrong, most of the time it is a good thing. The Father wants to hear from His children. Worship, prayer, and fellowship are all wonderful things that honor the heart of God. But sometimes I wonder if we have under-estimated the power of silence. When is the last time you have been in the presence of God and not said a word? Have you ever been moved so much that you feared saying a word might quench the moment?

I remember playing at a retreat several years ago for a youth group of about five hundred students. The youth pastor wanted us to play all the fast songs we knew to really get the kids going. So needless to say, when it was time to go into a more intimate time of worship, everyone was bouncing off the walls! I stepped back from the microphone, not really sure what to do next because they were so out of control. I started praying for a little help and was suddenly reminded of Psalm 46:10, "Be still and know that I am God." I went to the microphone and yelled over the crowd, "The best way for you to worship right now is to sit down and shut up!" Not very orthodox, I know, but what happened next was amazing.

In about two seconds the room got quiet. I mean really quiet! You could have heard a pin drop. We sat there in silence for about fifteen minutes or so. There was an incredible sense of reverence that came over that place. It was one of the most intense times of worship I have ever experienced, and not a word was spoken, not a song was sung.

Why? What made it so special? Because corporate worship is not only about being heard by God, but hearing God as well. If we continue making all the noise and not taking the time to hear from the Father, we risk the chance of forgetting why we started making noise in the first place. If I told my wife I loved her and never gave her a chance to respond, I would begin to wonder how she felt. If a conversation with my wife consisted of me doing all the talking and her never getting a chance to say anything, our relationship would fall apart. All relationships are based on two-way communication, and our relationship with Christ, being the ultimate relationship, is obviously no different.

So next time you find yourself in a time of worship, take a moment to be silent. Since we are so good at talking, stop and ask the Father to speak to you. Be reminded that Christ sings over you! Be reminded that the King of kings has called you by name! I promise you, it will make the sweetest times of worship so much sweeter.

Be silent for more than a moment and listen to what God is speaking to you right now, at this very hour of time. If we recognize that He sometimes even speaks through silence, what is His message to you now?

_____

_____

_____

_____

_____

_____

_____

_____

_____

_____

_____

_____

_____

_____

_____

_____

_____

BELIEVE

"Lord! we know what we are, but know not what we may be."

William Shakespeare

LORD MOST HIGH
Don Harris & Gary Sadler

From the ends of the earth
From the depths of the sea
From the heights of the heavens
Your name be praised

From the hearts of the weak
From the shouts of the strong
From the lips of all people
This song we raise Lord

Throughout the endless ages
You will be crowned with praises
Lord Most High
Exalted in every nation
Sovereign of all creation
Lord Most High
Be magnified

Eleven

In the 1980s on movie screens everywhere, Marty McFly jumped into a revamped Delorean time machine and accidentally ended up a live spectator and participant in his 1950s parents' lives. He spends the better part of the film trying to find a way back to the future, but in the midst of it all ends up toying enough with the time-space continuum to make his old life a much better place to return to. Not a bad gig if you can get it.

Ask anyone today where they'd choose to go if given the opportunity to hop in a time machine, and surprisingly few take it up for the get-rich or change-your-life schemes that such a trip would make possible. The answer I've always heard, including my own, would be to go somewhere around Galilee at the time Jesus was walking those sands. But unlike the movies, which make everything seem easy, the harsh reality is that even if science and magic could transport you there, you wouldn't understand a single word anyone (including Jesus) was saying once you arrived. Not to mention the Levi's and tennis

> **My suspicion is, you wouldn't want to look suspicious in first-century Palestine.**

shoes and any other 21st-century accoutrements that would make one a pretty visible target for suspicion.

My suspicion is, you wouldn't want to look suspicious in first-century Palestine. So in the worst-case scenario, you'd likely end up dead or locked up. In the best of situations, you might melt into the crowd. Even when you ran into Jesus or any of the disciples, you'd drive yourself mad trying to make everyone understand who you were and what you were doing there.

That dream still haunts all of us, though—that great "if only." *If only I could see Jesus face to face; talk to Him; ask Him just what He means by all those things He's saying. To know once and for all what each little mystery meant . . .*

LIKE PILATE WE'VE ALL
WANTED TO LOOK INTO JESUS'
EYES AND ASK, "WHAT IS TRUTH?

Like Pilate we've all wanted to look into His eyes and ask, "What is truth?" Yes, we're sure we know by the scatterings of proof that we've picked up along our way. But nothing could be finer than actually standing before the Creator of the universe and asking once and for all the colossal, unanswerable questions.

With two thousand years between the dream and the reality (and the hope of a time machine not really looking that promising), Jesus still offers us access to Him—the God of yesterday, today, and tomorrow—and welcomes us wherever and whenever we want. His invitation still stands today: "Come unto me." And when you do, He promises you the time of your life.

*If you could step beyond the bounds of prayer
and stand face to face with the Lord to ask or
say one thing to Him, what would it be?*

_____

_____

_____

_____

_____

_____

_____

_____

_____

_____

_____

_____

_____

_____

_____

_____

_____

_____

_____

REMEMBER

"There is a land of the living and a land of the dead and the only bridge is love, the only survival, the only meaning."

Thornton Wilder

IN THAT DAY
Joseph Sabolick

My heart's burning for that day
When I'll see You face to face
I'll keep watching and waiting
Staying focused on Your Word

I will see You
I will touch You
You will hold me
In that day

My heart's burning for that day
When I'll see You face to face
There's a longing in my soul
To hear You say well done

Twelve

I was five years old when I stood beside my mother at an open grave as she said good-bye to her own mother. I barely understood any of what was going on, but I knew somehow that our world had changed forever. I had never seen so many people so sad.

Throughout the ceremony my mother held in her hand a flower given to her from the wealth of flowers covering the coffin. She clung to it as tightly as to my hand, and when the final, final moment came and we watched that box sink slowly into the ground, she stepped forward for one last look. And then I watched as she held out the bright flower, debated keeping this one symbol, and then, in a streak of orange, threw it into the dark before her. In slow motion I watched her let go of that last chance to hold on to a moment . . . to keep a token of what was. I have never forgotten actually feeling the piece of her heart that fell inside with the flower.

Even when the end is before us and we know the darkness has come, we still reach out with one last touch, one last hope of pushing back that inevitable dying of the light. It is so hard to let go that we strive for any way to hold on for even just one minute longer.

EVEN WHEN THE END IS BEFORE US AND WE KNOW THE DARKNESS HAS COME, WE STILL REACH OUT WITH ONE LAST TOUCH, ONE LAST HOPE OF PUSHING BACK THAT INEVITABLE DYING OF THE LIGHT.

Twelve

Annie Dillard wrote, "And you can get caught holding one end of a love, when your father drops, and your mother; when a land is lost, or a time . . . you reel out love's long line alone, stripped like a live wire loosed in space to longing and grief everlasting."

We've all held the one end of a love and been left in that desolate aloneness. Death is the ultimate portrait, but there are, too, those little deaths of our everyday life—broken hearts, lost dreams, vanished hopes—that also put us face to face with the empty-handedness of our days.

The composer Chopin called Warsaw his home, but in the end, asked that though his body be buried in Poland, his heart would be set in the ground of Paris. In his final wishes lay the desire to remain touching what most touched his heart in life. To be where your heart loved—home or abroad, inside or out, near to everything that filled your soul with joy—is the core of human desire.

Even when we are left behind, we are never alone. A piece of everyone we have ever loved will always be a part

TO BE WHERE YOUR HEART LOVED
IS THE CORE OF HUMAN DESIRE.

of us. So is Jesus, who left with us the greatest promise of all against the loneliest of nights: "I am with you always, even to the end of the world."

God is the ultimate Healer of our sorrows, and He promised to bear our griefs with us. What reminders do you have around you of never being left alone, even while letting go of someone you loved?

_____

_____

_____

_____

_____

_____

_____

_____

_____

_____

_____

_____

_____

_____

_____

_____

_____

_____

_____

CELEBRATE

"The boundary lines have fallen for me in pleasant places;
surely I have a delightful inheritance."

Psalm 16:6

FREEDOM
Darrell Evans

Where the Spirit of the Lord is
There is freedom
Where the Spirit of the Lord is
There is freedom
There is peace there is love
There is joy

It is for freedom You've set us free
It is for freedom You've set us free
I'm free I'm free
I'm free I'm free

So we will walk in Your freedom
Walk in Your liberty
We will walk in Your freedom
Walk in Your liberty
We will dance in Your freedom
Dance in Your liberty
We will dance in Your freedom
Dance in Your liberty

Being a libertarian does inherently have some perks, but you have to believe that after a few weeks of doing anything you ever wanted to do without fear of consequences, the nov-

> YOU HAVE TO BELIEVE THAT
> AFTER A FEW WEEKS OF DOING
> ANYTHING YOU WANT WITHOUT
> FEAR OF CONSEQUENCES, THE
> NOVELTY MIGHT BEGIN
> TO WEAR OFF.

elty might begin to wear off. The idea of laws seems at once to be coldhearted and a killjoy to anyone seeking the true pleasures of life, but without laws, the consequences might be even colder. Someone once explained it like this:

Picture a group of children playing on a mountain-high plateau. Everything's perfect—playmates, sunshine, grass to run through. But one false step near the rim of this plateau and they'll be tumbling down a sheer cliff.

You can imagine what happens. No one can truly enjoy the "playground"—the kids can run, but not too far. Fear of falling off the edge consumes most of their moments, making playtime not so carefree. When the sun sets, they're even less likely to venture anywhere past the center of the plateau. Fear limits all movement.

But then, let someone construct a wall around the perimeter and watch what happens. With the protection of the wall, play again becomes free. The children can run as fast as they want. They twirl, spin, skip, fly, and have no fear of falling over the edge. There is a boundary there to hold them in. Ironic as it sounds, the wall does set them free.

That's the wall God built. The psalmist understood it well, constantly celebrating the liberation of the laws while those around him decried their bondage. He discovered the secret: He knew that the Law was not created to appease a

GOD'S WAYS WERE TRULY THE PATH
TO LIVING FREE, AND NOT JUST A
GRUMPY OLD MAN'S UNREASONABLE
DEMANDS ON ALL THE ANNOYING
NEIGHBORHOOD KIDS.

fickle God, but rather to create a security that led to life. He didn't see a barrier to joy but a bridge to a fully experienced life. God's ways were truly the path to living free, and not just a grumpy old man's unreasonable demands on all the annoying neighborhood kids.

"Eat, drink, and be merry, for tomorrow we die" may seem like a fun way to go, but in the long run, the casualties of sin far outweigh the burden of law abiding. Simply put, life is a lot more worth living when set inside the arms of the Law Giver. His laws, steeped in love and wrapped in mercy, give all those who follow Him more joy than any adventure "past the wall" could ever offer.

Robert Frost wrote that "good fences make good neighbors"—presumably knowing that keeping things out is what makes for peace. But in God's landscaping, keeping us safely inside His Word and His world is what truly makes for peace. The true, lasting peace found only inside the freedom of those walls that Love built.

*Reflect on God's Word and the ways His "laws"
have guided you in your life. Which have you
struggled to keep and which have set you free?*

_____

_____

_____

_____

_____

_____

_____

_____

_____

_____

_____

_____

_____

_____

_____

_____

_____

_____

L E A R N

"I know that you can do all things;
no plan of yours can be thwarted."

Job 42:2

BETTER THAN LIFE
Cindy Cruse Ratcliff & Israel Houghton

Your love is everlasting
It's an everlasting love
Mercy is as new as every rising of the sun
And Your loving kindness
Loving kindness is better than life

Your grace is all sufficient
It's an all-sufficient grace
The power and Your glory are forever on display
And Your loving kindness
Loving kindness is better than life

Fairest of ten thousand
Of ten thousand You are fair
Nothing in this world could ever measure or compare
And Your loving kindness
Loving kindness is better than life

Reality TV. I'm hooked. I know they say it's a fad, but I for one hope it doesn't go away too soon.

I do have some limits: I like the classics. Forget the wanna-bes that make contestants eat all manner of inedibles and then dump a basket of worms on top of their heads. I prefer the conniving, plotting, scheming fun of the shows that pit person

I MARVEL WATCHING WHAT
PEOPLE DO ON THESE SHOWS,
ONLY TO DISCOVER THEY'RE A
PERFECT MIRROR OF EVERYTHING
I'VE DONE THE WEEK BEFORE.

against person, brain against brain, and righteous indignation against righteous indignation.

It's a great life lesson. I marvel watching what people do on these shows, only to discover they're a perfect mirror of everything I've done the week before. My adventures might not include immunity idols and races through fire and water, but the heart of the matter is constant. We're all guilty of incredibly bad behavior in the face of our pursuits.

In his own version of reality TV, the prophet Nathan told King David a story that would have made for a great night's ratings. Look, he said, there was a town with two families—one very poor and the other very rich. The poor family owned a lamb, more of a pet than a plain old farm animal. This family loved that lamb with all their hearts, even letting their little bundle of wool sleep and eat right in the house. One day the rich family got some unexpected company, and instead of running out for some decent take-out to impress the guests, the man of the house grabbed the lamb right from under the poor family's nose. Dinner was served.

David was outraged and demanded that the rich man be immediately voted off the island for his heinous act. What Israel's king failed to see was the not-so-thin disguise Nathan put on the main character in the story. Incredulous at David's thick-headedness in the face of so clear a picture of his own recent exploits (which included stealing the love and the life of poor Uriah), Nathan very well may have even shouted: "You are the man!"—and under his breath (or possibly out loud, considering the circumstance), " . . . you dumb clod."

It's easy to see the ridiculousness of the antics of someone else; but turn the mirror on you, and most of the time you barely recognize yourself, let alone your shenanigans.

Sometimes it takes seeing things outside ourselves to realize what we've been doing inside ourselves all along.

Oddly, most of the Bible's best tales involve the people who are "just like us"—ordinary people in extraordinary cir-

> SOMETIMES IT TAKES SEEING
> THINGS OUTSIDE OURSELVES
> TO REALIZE WHAT WE'VE
> BEEN DOING INSIDE
> OURSELVES ALL ALONG.

cumstances who, in the end, usually act just as we would. For better or worse, no matter what any of them or any of us do, in the final scene we all get to come one step closer to Him. And that's worth more than any prize a month in the jungle could ever get you.

What secrets are you keeping hidden in your life? How is God showing you ways to reveal and deal with them?

_____

_____

_____

_____

_____

_____

_____

_____

_____

_____

_____

_____

_____

_____

_____

_____

_____

_____

_____

WATCH

*"The heavens declare the glory of God;
the skies proclaim the work of his hands."*

Psalm 19:1

I WORSHIP YOU ALMIGHTY GOD
Sandra Corbett-Wood

*I worship You Almighty God
There is none like You
I worship You O Prince of Peace
That is what I want to do
I give You praise
For You are my righteousness
I worship You Almighty God
There is none like You*

Genesis was only the beginning. God started creating on day one and hasn't stopped since. And from what anyone can tell, He's not slowing down yet.

Only God can make a tree, not to mention the million other things He creates and recreates every day the sun rises on His handiwork. His mercies really are new every morning. And His creativity never ends. According to the painter Picasso, "God is really only another artist. He invented the giraffe, the

> ONE CAN ALMOST SEE HIM
> AS THE WILD-EYED ARTIST,
> FLINGING HIS ART WHEREVER
> HIS WHIMS TOSS IT.

elephant, and the cat. He has no real style. He just goes on trying other things."

One can almost see Him as the wild-eyed artist, fling-
ing His art wherever His whims toss it; creating anything and

> HE'LL CREATE ANYTHING
> AND ANYONE HE WANTS,
> AND HE'LL DO THE SAME WITH
> HIS LOVE. HE'LL LET IT RAIN
> DOWN ON ANYONE, ANYWHERE.

everything that His heart desires and that His hands can shape.
He's certainly not worried about the critics. If he wants to
make something, no one and no thing can stop Him.

His love is just as wild. Sometimes you'd think He

doesn't even stop to think about it. He'll create anything and anyone He wants, and He'll do the same with His love. He'll let it rain down on anyone, anywhere.

Back in the '70s, one of the popular happy-face buttons found on people's lapels happily exclaimed, "Smile! God Loves You!" Commenting on their appeal, someone once said that though the buttons seemed a nice sentiment, they really proved nothing more than the fact that "God has no taste." Or at least no discretion. His love just falls anywhere and everywhere. It's not even presumptuous to assume that everyone you bump into, God loves. In fact, He'd probably dare you to bump into someone He *didn't*. You'd be walking an awfully long time.

God never gives up. God never stops. His creativity knows no bounds and His love has no limits. He'll keep making a new thing as long as His people are there to enjoy it. And whether you want Him to or not, he'll continue a good work in you and a good work in His world. He'll splash beauty all around, just for you, in his never-ending quest to win your heart, for He is "powerless" when it comes to love—He just can't resist it.

Just look around you and see.

How hard is it for you to believe God really does love you?
Think of the ways He has tried to show you today.

_____

_____

_____

_____

_____

_____

_____

_____

_____

_____

_____

_____

_____

_____

_____

_____

_____

WORSHIP

"And they sang a new song: 'You are worthy
to take the scroll and to open its seals because . . .
with your blood you purchased men for God.'"

Revelation 5:9

WORTHY IS THE LAMB
Darlene Zschech

Thank You for the cross Lord
Thank You for the price You paid
Bearing all my sin and shame
In love You came
And gave amazing grace

Thank You for this love Lord
Thank You for the nail-pierced hands
Washed me in Your cleansing flow
Now all I know
Your forgiveness and embrace

Worthy is the Lamb
Seated on the throne
Crown You now with many crowns
You reign victorious
High and lifted up
Jesus Son of God
The darling of heaven crucified
Worthy is the Lamb
Worthy is the Lamb

"Worthy" was inspired through a beautiful antique hymnal that was found in an equally–as–ancient bookstore in Wales. I found myself poring over these mostly majestic songs (as some were quite depressing!) ... and found the theme of the cross woven throughout many of the lyrics, just page after page.

I was reminded yet again that the only reason I stand justified today is because of the power of the cross ... the reality of the sacrifice, the reality of the overwhelming love of humanity in the Father's heart and all He was willing to give to set us free.

The lyric "Thank you for the cross" seemed too sim-plistic for a song, but honestly, it's what I wanted to say. If there is one thing I desire to remain in life, it is THANKFUL. The true heart of a "praiser" is a thankful heart ... and sometimes, in a world atmosphere of getting more, wanting more, and feeling incomplete without more, we can so easily run into every day without remembering how far we have already come.

Wake up in the morning, look toward heaven, and say THANK YOU!! Just remember your "BC" life (Before Christ!); you'll find yourself praising before you know it!

The chorus flowed quite quickly, as Revelation 5 is never far from my mind—the thought of thousands upon tens of thousands of angels circling the magnificent throne of our King, singing, "Worthy is the Lamb", and then EVERY creature in Heaven and on earth joining in to sing, "To Him who sits on the throne, and to the Lamb ... praise, honor, glory, and power for ever!!" This anthem of love being proclaimed throughout Heaven and earth is too wonderful to try and describe, but needless to say, continues to have a powerful effect on me.

The line "Crown you now with many crowns" paints a powerful picture, as when the soldiers twisted together the ultimate mockery in the form of a crown of thorns and embedded it in the head of our Savior, saying, "Hail, King of the Jews"; well, the agony ringing throughout all of Heaven is too much to comprehend.

But Revelation 19 describes the return of our Lord, the crown of thorns replaced with MANY crowns—crowns of victory and splendor ... the King of kings ... He reigns victorious!

Dear friends, I pray that you never forget the price that has been paid for you, and that you live understanding that you are not for sale; you are treasured beyond words. The Word declares many times that God Himself crowns us as heirs of the throne, with splendor, righteousness, blessing, salvation, love, and compassion . . . the list goes on and on. Worship and honor Him with your life today. It is the very least we can do!

Your Worship Adventure

God is worthy to be praised. How do you show this truth to others through your own life?

_____

_____

_____

_____

_____

_____

_____

_____

_____

_____

_____

_____

_____

_____

_____

_____

_____

_____

_____

LIVE

"Life itself is the most wonderful fairy tale."

Hans Christian Andersen

YOU ARE GOOD
Israel Houghton

Lord You are good
And Your mercy endureth forever
Lord You are good
And Your mercy endureth forever

People from every nation and tongue
From generation to generation

We worship You
Hallelujah
Hallelujah
We worship You
For who You are

We worship You
You are good
All the time
All the time
You are good

Cinderella may have believed that "a dream is a wish your heart makes," but (in the Disney version, anyway) it took a whole lot of elbow grease and the ingenuity of a flock of little birds and sportily clad mice to really make those dreams come true.

"The Lord helps those who help themselves," urged Benjamin Franklin, and even in fairy tales, when a whole lot of magic is on hand for the using, that truth still stands. You've got to be willing to work hard if you want to start living the life you've only imagined.

Jack had a lot of climbing to do before he got his golden egg, and Eliza Doolittle had to put in more hours than there were in a day before she could become anyone's fair lady. Even Jacob, who among his many dreams held out hope for a love and life with Rachel, had to work an unenviably long shift with his soon-to-be father-in-law. After sweating seven

> EVEN IN FAIRY TALES, WHEN
> A WHOLE LOT OF MAGIC IS
> ON HAND FOR THE USING,
> YOU'VE STILL GOT TO BE WILLING
> TO WORK HARD IF YOU WANT
> TO START LIVING THE LIFE
> YOU'VE ONLY IMAGINED.

years to win her hand, he was tricked into another seven years of back-breaking labor before he could actually ride off into the sunset with his beloved. But in the equation of love, he still knew he came out ahead. Jacob might have even claimed it would've been worth another seven years of trickery just to win this princess of his heart.

"Happily ever after" would be even more so if only it came down from on high—on a silver tray, bed of roses, or any other comfortable conveyance. At least that seems like the best ending. But the reality is, the rocky road toward the storybook finish is what truly creates the worthwhile life. "Dream and become" is a promise with a price. Anything of value is.

> "DREAM AND BECOME" IS A
> PROMISE WITH A PRICE.
> ANYTHING OF VALUE IS.

Thoreau acknowledged that building castles in the air was not a waste of time. In fact, it was a perfectly fine way to dream. But it also means you have to work to build the foundation underneath. In other words, even when life gives you a fairy tale, you still must remain an asker, seeker, and knocker.

The work of dream-making is never done. Because when all is said and done and every story plays out to its inevitable end, the important thing is this: Not just to live happily ever after—but to *live*.

Are your dreams so unattainable that all they'll ever be is dreams? What are the reachable goals you can set today to bring you closer to the "coming true"?

_____

_____

_____

_____

_____

_____

_____

_____

_____

_____

_____

_____

_____

_____

_____

_____

_____

_____

IMAGINE

"How wonderful it is that nobody need wait a single moment before starting to improve the world."

Anne Frank

ARISE KING OF KINGS
Mick Goss Becky Heaslip & Eoghan Heaslip

We call upon Your name O Lord
The name that is holy

We call upon Your name O Lord
We come to bring our praise to the One
Who was, Who is and is to come

Arise King of kings
God of all creation
O Lord we cry
Arise King of kings
Father to the nations
The Rock of our salvation
O God arise

Martin Luther King had a dream. And he carried that dream from a tiny little church in the South and somehow ended up setting the world on fire with it. But not without a whole lot of trouble along the way. Inspired by the words of Gandhi and buoyed by an unshakable belief that God had indeed created all men equal, King had no choice but to shake up everyone and everything around him until they, too, could see the truth.

It has been said that it is better to light one small candle than to curse the darkness. When night completely

HE ENDED UP FOOLING
EVERYBODY USING A WEAPON
NO ONE EXPECTED — LOVE.

surrounded him, King struck that match and spoke *to* the darkness, not against it. He started a war without picking up a gun, and fought against tyrants without stooping to any of their tactics. "Darkness," he once said, "cannot drive out hate; only love can do that." And he ended up fooling everybody using a weapon no one expected—love. Not just love as an idea, but love at any cost.

With history now behind us, it seems inevitable that what he preached was possible and that of course, love was the way. But to be in the middle of that tempest took every ounce of courage a man could muster and a dream bigger than anyone could destroy.

John Lennon wrote a song inviting people to join him in a hope that one day there would be no color, no religion, no countries; to imagine a world where living together as one was more important than living for the things that tear us apart. Dr. King grasped that hope a decade earlier when he forced the world to look at itself the way God looks at it: as all of His children seeking the way Home.

Taking it one step further, King resorted to the most amazing tactic of all—forgiveness. "The weak never forgive," said Gandhi, himself a designer of peaceful weaponry. "Forgiveness is an attribute of the strong." Knowing he was forgiven by the

DR. KING GRASPED THAT HOPE A DECADE EARLIER WHEN HE FORCED THE WORLD TO LOOK AT ITSELF THE WAY GOD LOOKS AT IT: AS ALL OF HIS CHILDREN SEEKING THE WAY HOME.

Lord of the universe allowed Martin Luther King to forgive those who begged to be left without forgiveness. He literally forgave until it hurt because he knew the truth: Only in love

ONLY IN LOVE AND FORGIVENESS
DO WE FIND FREEDOM. AND ONLY
IN FREEDOM DO WE LIVE IN THE
EVERLASTING ARMS OF GOD.

and forgiveness do we find freedom. And only in freedom do we live in the everlasting arms of God.

Thank God for that promise, and thank God for His peace. And thank God Almighty we *are* free at last.

On earth, freedom is always bought at a great price, but God freely gives it to us in our lives. What do you most appreciate about your freedom—both the freedom of where you live and the freedom God gives you through His Spirit?

_____

_____
_____
_____
_____
_____
_____
_____
_____
_____
_____
_____
_____
_____
_____
_____
_____
_____
_____

PRAY

"Call to me and I will answer you and tell you great and unsearchable things you do not know."

Jeremiah 33:3

COME JUST AS YOU ARE
Joseph Sabolick

Come just as you are
Hear the Spirit call
Come just as you are
Come and see, come receive
Come and live forever

Life everlasting
And strength for today
Taste the Living Water
And never thirst again

Nineteen

"Prayer changes things" is a message seen on everything from needlepoint pillows to bumper stickers, bookmarks, and t-shirts. I'm not sure we've ever really stopped to think about it, though. Does praying something really make it so? And would we really want to believe in a God who worked that way? Sure,

> DOES PRAYING SOMETHING
> REALLY MAKE IT SO?
> AND WOULD WE REALLY
> WANT TO BELIEVE IN A GOD
> WHO WORKED THAT WAY?

you might know the best things to ask for and the right way to do it, but what about the guy next to you whose requests may very well screw up your own?

It's like praying for your team to win the Super Bowl. It's the ultimate divine showdown. Both teams also prayed for the trophy. Which one did God decide prayed harder? Or better? Or with more fans in a sheer numbers game? It's ludicrous. And yet we still, with hearts pure and true, pour out our requests to God and wonder why He doesn't seem to answer.

When Jesus said, "This is how you should pray," He was letting us in on one of the secrets. It's not a shopping list; it's a

WHEN JESUS SAID, "THIS IS
HOW YOU SHOULD PRAY,"
HE WAS LETTING US IN
ON ONE OF THE SECRETS.

conversation. It's not Santa Claus . . . it's your Father. God knows what you want before you ask. You're not letting Him in on anything new. He knows you need that job, that you want the test to come back negative, that you hope the check somehow won't bounce. I even believe He cares enough to walk you through the most minor of your day's concerns.

What counts is that He hears from you—and that you're willing to call. And He asks you to listen. The trick is learning to listen and hear the answer He wants, not the one you do. "If you begin to live life looking for the God that is all around you," writes Frank Bianco, "every moment becomes a prayer."

There's the hardest lesson of all. Just like the little children we were and the little children we still are, it's so much easier even now to just ask and ask and ask—and sometimes to beg and beg and beg for everything we want. As our Father, He will sit and patiently hear us out—but as He's tried so many times to teach us and show us, all He really wants to hear is our voice. He just asks that we begin that conversation with Him, that intimate, loving, trusting, tender kind of dialogue usually reserved for lovers or children—and that the conversation should never end.

*Have you ever tried to pray without asking for anything?—
even prayed for the ability to do so? Listen to
what God says to your heart when you speak to Him,
not as a giver, but as a friend.*

TRUST

"You will keep in perfect peace him whose mind is steadfast, because he trusts in you."

Isaiah 26:3

ONLY A GOD LIKE YOU
Tommy Walker

Only a God like You
Could be worthy of my praise
And all my hope and faith
To only a King of all kings
Do I bow my knee and sing
Give my everything

To only my Maker, my Father, my Savior
Redeemer, restorer
Rebuilder, rewarder
To only a God like You
Do I give my praise

Twenty

P. T. Barnum said there was one born every minute. A sucker, that is. I took the sixty seconds of an early May morning. I think I'm one of only three people in the world who actually grabbed a dictionary to prove 'em wrong when someone said, "Did you know they forgot to put the word 'gullible' in the dictionary?"

IT WASN'T A STRETCH TO THINK THAT IF YOU ACTUALLY MADE IT TO THE END OF THE RAINBOW, THERE'D BE A WHOLE LOT OF GOLD FOR THE TAKING.

I believed in Santa Claus for eight long years. I knew that if you dug that hole deep enough, you would end up in the middle of China. It wasn't a stretch to think that if you actually made it to the end of the rainbow, there'd be a whole lot of gold for the taking. And a talking cricket was just as good a source as any to prove that when you wish upon a star, your dreams come true.

Doubting Thomas earned his eternal nickname for presumably not being that easy to dupe. He wasn't about to believe the first thing he heard. And if what everyone was shouting about was real, he'd believe it just as soon as it stood right in front of him. Sort of the ultimate "yeah, right" that echoes through the ages. Lucky for Thomas, Jesus had a soft spot for those stoic, hard-to-believe souls and let Thomas see and touch to his heart's content.

"Blessed are those who believe without seeing," Jesus said. But somehow you knew it wasn't an indictment of Thomas as much as a marvel that there might be an unfettered circle of believers who'd risk their hearts on everything without tangible proof.

LUCKY FOR THOMAS, JESUS HAD
A SOFT SPOT FOR THOSE STOIC,
HARD-TO-BELIEVE SOULS AND
LET THOMAS SEE AND TOUCH TO
HIS HEART'S CONTENT.

Jesus may have seemed like the circus huckster trying to trick the rabble to enter the tent, but the truth was, He was ready to put on a sideshow of enormous proportions. You could even go so far as to say He ended up putting on the greatest show on earth.

However, there is one thing we can know and trust: The God of wonders never suckers anyone into anything. He came, He saw, and He conquered every heart that was willing to listen to what He had to say. And when He's the one doing the talking, you *know* you can believe it. Because He's never made a promise He couldn't keep.

Do you find yourself trusting in God only when it is the obvious thing to do? What are the circumstances in your life that can draw you closer to Him even when His presence is not so clear?

_____

_____

_____

_____

_____

_____

_____

_____

_____

_____

_____

_____

_____

_____

_____

_____

_____

_____

B E

"God moves in mysterious ways, His wonders to perform."

William Cowper

THERE IS NONE LIKE YOU
Lenny LeBlanc

There is none like You
No one else can touch
My heart like You do
I could search
For all eternity long and find
There is none like You

Twenty-One

When Dr. Frankenstein built the monster that became his namesake out of an assortment of parts, even he couldn't have imagined the triumph and the tragedy that would come of his creation. Triumph because he had entered into the realm

PERHAPS AFTER ALL, CREATING
LIFE IS BEST LEFT TO GOD.

of the divine—bringing life out of nothingness. Tragedy because, perhaps after all, creating life is best left to God.

Not that mankind hasn't made it a habit to dabble in God's realm. Thinking that just maybe we can do Him one better, we have all given it a try at least once. And like the mythological Icarus who wanted to fly to the gods, we've donned our man-made wings, only to fly too close to the sun and come plummeting back to the earth in a ball of feathers and melted wax. And still just as far as we ever were from reaching that elusive desire—to see God, to know God, to be God.

"You created my inmost being; you knit me together in my mother's womb," wrote the psalmist. Surely we should trust that the One who built us each out of nothing requires nothing more than our love in return. Yet day in and day out

SURELY WE SHOULD TRUST
THAT THE ONE WHO BUILT
US EACH OUT OF NOTHING
REQUIRES NOTHING MORE
THAN OUR LOVE IN RETURN.

we search for more ways to find Him who has been near to us all along. Or we even go so far as to actually try to create

Him—in our own image, just the way we want or need Him to be. They are all futile efforts, though—as outrageous as the clay trying to mold the potter.

Like Dr. Frankenstein, who burst into tears of joy when he zapped the monstrosity on his table into being, it's impos-

> IT'S IMPOSSIBLE TO IMAGINE
> THE CONSEQUENCES OUR
> GREAT PLANS MAY BRING.

sible to imagine the consequences our great plans may bring. Few of us begin with a heart bent on destruction. But that is what Frankenstein's creation eventually wrought. He believed he had captured the secret power of life and became his own little god. We do the same every time we try to recreate God into the god we think He should be.

God created the world and everything in it. If we can't trust Him to run it, our only other choice is to rely on our own created monstrosities—our own patchwork of what He should do, and be, for us. Unleashed upon the world—or even just our own little worlds—that's a creation that is just too frightening to fathom.

How have you tried to recreate God in your own image?
Remind yourself of the joy you've experienced
when you've entrusted God with your life plan.

_____

_____

_____

_____

_____

_____

_____

_____

_____

_____

_____

_____

_____

_____

_____

_____

_____

_____

_____

_____

SURRENDER

"Now then," said Joshua, *"throw away the foreign gods that are among you and yield your hearts to the LORD, the God of Israel."*

Joshua 24:23

I WILL
Rick Heil & Todd Shay

*My Savior Redeemer
My love and my Lord
I give You all of my heart
My will and my soul
You take me as I am
A scarred and broken man
Lord I surrender all I have to You to You
I will give You everything I will I will
Make my life an offering
I will I will*

*I will give You everything
I will I will
Make my life an offering
I will I will
I will give my heart to You
I will I will
Broken and poured out for You
I will I will*

"Father, if you are willing, take this cup from me;
yet *not my will,* but yours be done" (Luke 22:41, emphasis
added) . . . is the most beautiful statement in the Bible. It's
from our Savior's lips right before He surrendered Himself

FROM THAT PLACE OF

TOTAL OBEDIENCE CAME

A HEART WILLING TO PLEASE

THE FATHER, NO MATTER

WHAT THE COST . . . EVEN IF

IT MEANT DEATH ON THE CROSS.

to be the greatest sacrifice of all time. From that place of
total obedience came a heart willing to please the Father,
no matter what the cost . . . even if it meant death on the
cross. And by that will, we have been made holy through

the sacrifice of the body of Jesus Christ once for all (Hebrews 10:10).

Surrendering our heart, soul, mind, and strength to the Lord in every sense of the word is a difficult task. It has been an ongoing challenge in my life ever since I knew right from wrong. The spirit is willing but the flesh is weak, and my evil desire has been to put myself first. My needs. My wants. I've even justified my selfishness as a way to deal with a disease I was diagnosed with when I was eleven years old.

I watched myself become very self-absorbed and learned that society teaches to "always look out for number one," and "if you don't look out for yourself, no one will." While on the other hand the Lord teaches that "the greatest among you should be like the youngest, and the one who rules like the one who serves" (Luke 22:26). Therefore, as we grow in Christ, we understand that the Lord has a higher call for our lives: to make Him the center of our existence while living a surrendered life to His will, not our own.

While becoming more like Christ is a lifetime process, accepting Him as our Savior is an immediate change of course,

AS WE GROW IN CHRIST,
WE UNDERSTAND THAT
THE LORD HAS A HIGHER
CALL FOR OUR LIVES.

for from that moment on we are made new by the blood of Jesus! Our surrender and total devotion is in response to His mercy and amazing grace. The moment we give our lives to the Lord, He calls us holy just as He called the Israelites holy once they were set free from the bondage of Egypt (Jeremiah 2:3). We have not earned our holiness, because it cannot be earned. Our holiness is what the Lord has predestined for His people, and it has come by the greatest sacrifice ever known to creation . . . the Creator Himself!

"Therefore, I urge you, brothers [and sisters], in view of God's mercy, to offer your bodies as living sacrifices, holy and pleasing to God — this is your spiritual act of worship. Do not conform any longer to the pattern of this world, but be transformed by the renewing of your mind. Then you will be able to test and approve what God's will is — his good, pleasing and perfect will" (Romans 12:1, 2).

May you be filled with the peace that comes from our Lord Jesus.

Surrendering wouldn't be considered a sacrifice if it were easy. What is the most difficult thing you have ever surrendered? Was the reward worth it?

_____

_____

_____

_____

_____

_____

_____

_____

_____

_____

_____

_____

_____

_____

_____

_____

_____

_____

GIVE

*"Nobody has ever measured, even poets,
how much a heart can hold."*

Zelda Fitzgerald

JESUS, YOU ARE
Rita Baloche

*Jesus, You are, You are
Everything I'm not
And everything that I want to be
Jesus, You are, You are
The Maker of my heart
Finish what You started in me*

*This is the hope I have
It's something I cannot see
You willingly gave Your life
Willing to die for me
Now I believe
I believe, I believe*

In *The Happy Prince,* Oscar Wilde tells the tale of a prince who is in fact a city statue, and of the little bird that befriends him. This strange pair love each other dearly, and in the process of their days, they manage to find ways to help the people around them. It's all done in secret, of course—who would even imagine that a little bird kibbitzing with a statue could affect anything at all? But affect they did.

Every night, at the prince's instruction, the bird would peck and peel off his friend's golden veneer and deliver the gold pieces to any pauper that could be found. When the gold was gone, the bird moved to the jewels on the prince's belt, his coat, his eyes. Eventually the statue ended up looking more like a monstrosity in the city's park rather than its glory, so the council voted to tear it down and start again with something beautiful. At least something beautiful in their eyes. Yet something more lovely, noble, and worthy than they could ever fashion themselves was right in front of their eyes.

SOMETHING MORE LOVELY,
NOBLE, AND WORTHY
THAN THEY COULD EVER
FASHION THEMSELVES WAS
RIGHT IN FRONT OF THEIR EYES.

As the days grew darker and colder, and the prince had less and less to give to the world, his little sparrow stood by his side. Abandoning the comfort of catching the flight southward with the rest of his flock, he instead chose to stick by his friend. The bird's loyalty and love cost him his life. Overcome by the cold, the sparrow died at the foot of the statue.

Without even noticing, the workmen tore down the prince and hauled away what could be melted and reformed, leaving behind what to them was nothing but garbage. But as

WHAT THEY LEFT BEHIND WAS
WORTH MORE THAN ALL THE
TREASURES OF HEAVEN.

Wilde pointed out, what they left behind was worth more than all the treasures of Heaven. There in the dust, forgotten by the world but alive forever in the eyes of God, was the broken iron heart of the prince and the cold, lifeless body of his truest feathered friend.

No greater love has any man, read the Scriptures, than to lay down his life for his friend. It is the ultimate gift offered by a few brave souls whose capacity for love exceeds their fear of that final defeat. And no one knows that equation better than

> TO LAY DOWN ONE'S LIFE FOR HIS FRIEND IS THE ULTIMATE GIFT OFFERED BY A FEW BRAVE SOULS WHOSE CAPACITY FOR LOVE EXCEEDS THEIR FEAR OF THAT FINAL DEFEAT.

God Himself. The Prince who stepped into His story claimed all of creation as His friend and offered Himself as the greatest giver of the greatest gift of all: His broken heart and His broken body—treasures that are worth more than the world's weight in gold.

*For what or who would you lay down your
very own life? What are ways you can spiritually
give your life for others every day?*

_____

_____

_____

_____

_____

_____

_____

_____

_____

_____

_____

_____

_____

_____

_____

_____

_____

_____

HOLD

"The only place outside of heaven where you can be perfectly safe from all the dangers of love is hell."

C. S. Lewis

I GIVE YOU MY HEART
Reuben Morgan

This is my desire
To honor You
Lord with all my heart
I worship You
All I have within me
I give You praise
All that I adore is in You

Lord I give You my heart
I give You my soul
I live for You alone
Ev'ry breath that I take
Ev'ry moment I'm awake
Lord have Your way in me

Twenty-Four

The noted writer and thinker C. S. Lewis once said, "To love at all is to be vulnerable." He was right. Every time you open your heart to someone or something new, you also

> EVERY TIME YOU OPEN YOUR HEART TO SOMEONE OR SOMETHING NEW, YOU ALSO INVITE THE CHANCE OF IT ALL GOING UTTERLY AND COMPLETELY WRONG.

invite the chance of it all going utterly and completely wrong. Deciding the gamble is worth it is, I suppose, the one thing that gets us all out of bed every morning.

I lost a beautiful pet early one autumn, and it took me

until the next spring to decide I was ready to welcome an-other little creature into my home. It certainly wasn't because it took me that long to forget the first pet; it took me that long to believe I could go through the pain again.

I cried all the way to where I was picking up this new little life—partly out of guilt that I had really let go of the other pet, partly because I knew I could never have her back again, and partly because three years, or ten years, or—hope against hope—twenty years down the road, I knew I'd have to say good-bye to this one too. And I just wasn't sure yet that the horrible day of farewell was something I was ready to invest in again. But as it is with all loves, the worth is not just in the number of days given to love but the moments of joy we can measure against it. The love itself is what it all comes down to.

There are no guarantees. Nothing lasts forever. Jesus

didn't even try to call it differently. "Blessed are they that mourn"? The only promise He gives here is one of comfort, not a promise for the mourned one's return.

> AS IT IS WITH ALL LOVES, THE
> WORTH IS NOT JUST IN THE
> NUMBER OF DAYS GIVEN TO LOVE
> BUT THE MOMENTS OF JOY WE
> CAN MEASURE AGAINST IT.

Love lost, though, is never truly lost. Love continues, transforms, and finds its home in any other place we open to its coming.

It's probably too much to presume animals understand the way things are and the risks that come with becoming a part of our lives—but that only makes the love they return all that more precious. An animal-lover once wrote of his amazement of this truth: When a cat has the choice of a feathered fireside bed, a rain-kissed garden patch, or a stream of glorious sunlight on a pillowsoft carpet—it will inevitably choose your lap as the one place it most wants to lay its head.

It's the ultimate picture of love. We all want to be held, cherished, known—and never be left alone. But even when the inevitable loss comes, more than anything, we want to know that we, too, once had that love. The kind of love that never dies.

What have you resisted opening your heart up to for fear of losing it? Ask God to give you the strength and wisdom to accept any gift of love that comes into your life.

_____

_____

_____

_____

_____

_____

_____

_____

_____

_____

_____

_____

_____

_____

_____

_____

_____

_____

_____

DECIDE

"The greatest way to live with honor in this world is to be what we pretend to be."

Socrates

RISE UP AND PRAISE HIM
Paul Baloche & Gary Sadler

Let the heavens rejoice
Let the earth be glad
Let the people of God
Sing His praise
All over the land
Everyone in the valley
Come and lift your voice
All those on the mountaintop
Be glad shout for joy

Rise up and praise Him
He deserves our love
Rise up and praise Him
Worship the Holy One
With all your heart
With all your soul
With all your might
Rise up and praise Him

W. W. J. D—What would Jesus do? At the risk of offending an entire industry of bracelets, t-shirts, books, and the like, I'd offer that that's not really the question. What Jesus would do might be determinable, but I doubt much of it would be emulatable. If we could do exactly what Jesus would do, we

> AS THE UN-DIVINE PEOPLE THAT
> WE ARE, WE'RE PRETTY MUCH
> STUCK WITH WHAT WE'VE GOT
> AND LEFT TO ASK THE MORE
> REALISTIC QUESTION: WHAT
> WOULD JESUS WANT ME TO DO?

wouldn't be the mere mortals that we are. Jesus Himself never even asked us to do *what* He did—He asked us to do *like* He did. As the un-divine people that we are, we're pretty much stuck with what we've got and left to ask the more realistic question: What would Jesus *want* me to do? Forget about thinking we could ever duplicate what Jesus did. When's the last time you gave sight back to the blind, fed a few thousand with one bag lunch, or forgave the sins of someone a pile of stones away from dying? It's just not doable. It wasn't even meant to be doable.

WHEN JESUS SAID, "YOU WILL DO EVEN GREATER THINGS THAN THESE"—HE WAS REFERRING TO THE POWER OF THE LOVE BEHIND HIS MIRACLES AND TEACHING.

When Jesus said, "You will do even greater things than these"—it seems He wasn't referring to His miracles, or to His teaching, but rather to the power of the love behind them.

I tend to think Jesus's stint on earth was less a show (although the program was spectacular, what with the healings and wine-makings and all) and more a sneak peek at the hope of what

> TO DO WHAT JESUS WOULD DO
> IS IMPOSSIBLE. BUT TO PUT
> OUR HEARTS AND LIVES INTO
> HIS HANDS IS NOT.

could be. "Follow me and I will make you," He said, "into what you can truly be." His ways are not our ways and His mind is unfathomable. To do what Jesus would do is impossible. But to put our hearts and lives into His hands is not.

"I am here to show you the way," He says. "Actually, I am the way." And His way is perfect. We can't even begin to become what He is, but He's not expecting that in the long run anyway. He came looking for hearts ready to try. Ready to try a new thing and discover that there is more to this life than trying to answer the question, especially when the answer really is right in front of our eyes.

Love is the only rule. And it's the one He asked us to live by. Let love be the one thing that determines the steps before you. I'm pretty sure that's just what Jesus would do.

Life is full of choices, and what you choose each day plays into what you will become. What will you do?

ACCEPT

"And we know that in all things God works
for the good of those who love him..."

Romans 8:28

I LOVE YOU LORD
Laurie Klein

I love You Lord
And I lift my voice
To worship You
O my soul rejoice
Take joy my King
In what You hear
May it be a sweet sweet sound
In Your ear

Perspective is everything. Like the woman who marveled at her husband thinking she was crazy for her choice of candidate during an election, when, as she described it, "He removes the hair in his nose by sticking a lit match up his nostril." Who really is the crazy one here?

WE PEOPLE HAVE FIGURED OUT
A ZILLION WAYS TO SET UP
AND STAKE OUT OUR
TERRITORIES. AND TO GUARD
THEM WITH OUR LIVES.

We spend most of our days thinking the inmates are running the asylum and we just need that one lucky break to make everything right again. Problem is, those same inmates are waiting for *us* to get back to our rooms. It all just depends on which way you look at it.

You don't have to go far to find a zillion ways we people have figured out to set up and stake out our own territories. And to guard them with our very lives. "This is the way things are." "What I'm saying is true." "I'm right and you're wrong." There is a marvelous comfort in believing what you believe is right while you wait for the rest of the world to catch up with you.

Reinhold Neibuhr described fanatic belief as something not actually rooted in faith but in doubt. "It is when we are not sure that we are doubly sure." And no one likes being around that someone who is doubly sure. "Methinks the lady doth protest too much," says Shakespeare's play of the queen who reeks with her own guilt. The loudest critics are sometimes the guiltiest, whether they're willing to admit it or not. It's easier to shoot down who you think is crazy than to examine the lunacy in your own life.

> THE LOUDEST CRITICS ARE
> SOMETIMES THE GUILTIEST,
> WHETHER THEY'RE WILLING
> TO ADMIT IT OR NOT.

God took the foolish things of the world and used them to confound the wise. You'd best be sure it isn't God talking, or an angel knocking at your door, before you close yourself off to the crazy thing—or the crazy one—beckoning.

Don't laugh someone off just because they don't live within your perspective, because from God's perspective it's all just a matter of trust. You could say He's not so much concerned with exactly what you believe, but with how you believe. A touch of grace never hurt anyone.

"Be not angry that you cannot make others as you wish them to be," warned Thomas á Kempis, "since you cannot make yourself as you wish to be." What consumes your heart will consume your life. Try to live and let live. And be glad God does the same with you.

Think about some of the issues in your life that you tend to argue about. As an exercise in perspective, try to argue with yourself from the other side. See what you discover about trying to truly understand others.

SEEK

"Life can only be understood backwards;
but it must be lived forwards."
Sören Kierkegaard

SHOUT TO THE NORTH
Martin Smith

Shout to the north and the south
Sing to the east and the west
Jesus is Savior to all
Lord of heaven and earth

Rise up church with broken wings
Fill this place with songs again
Of our God who reigns on high
By His grace again we'll fly

We've been through fire
We've been through rain
We've been refined
By the pow'r of His name
We've fallen deeper
In love with You
You've burned the truth on our lips

Lord of heaven and earth
Lord of heaven and earth
Lord of heaven and earth

In one of the legends of Arthur, that man who would be king began his journey to the throne with the unlikely name that belied his future greatness, Wart. And Wart's true-bluest

> HISTORY IS HINGED ON THE
> UNDYING BELIEF THAT MAN CAN
> SEEK AND FIND THE LIVING GOD.

companion was even more unlikely: the magnificent Merlin, a wizard living backward through time and ready to bestow the wisdom of the ages on his charge.

There between a lofty, magical beginning and a noble, heartbreaking ending are sandwiched the stories of how a boy becomes a man, how a heart becomes truly human, and how history is hinged on the undying belief that man can seek and find the living God.

With Merlin's extraordinary gift of what could be called the ultimate 20/20 hindsight and an intense belief in the nobility of man and the power of love, Arthur led a movement

ARTHUR BELIEVED THAT THE
QUEST FOR GOD IS LIFE'S MOST
NOBLE PURSUIT.

that still resonates in the hearts of man. He believed that not only was the quest for God life's most noble pursuit, but that leading people to that desire was the ultimate honor.

Twenty-Seven

The tales of the search for the holy grail that King Arthur is often regaled for initiating really all have at their core one goal: not just to find this mystical, possibly even magical, relic, but more so to discover each man's own knightly heart while in pursuit of it.

The holy grail represented nothing more than man's ever-arching ache to find a piece of God on earth. This precious cup that they believed Jesus drank from at the Last Supper spoke to these seekers as much more than just a souvenir from the Lord they served. In it, each of these pure-in-heart questers really knew they could touch the core of the One who owned their hearts. To be sure, most thought that the one who found this grail would also be bestowed with all the powers of Heaven—the power to heal, the power to lead, and the power to love. But whatever magic might have come with the discovery, as their king taught them, the true power actually came in the discovery of themselves while on the road *to* the treasure.

Arthur himself never did find that holy relic (though he inspired a nation and a wealth of people, as history has marched on). But as you read of this king's triumphs, somehow that particular failure didn't really matter. It didn't matter because it was, in the end, only a technical failure.

Merlin could have told him, no one really ever need find that elusive cup. It was, after all, just a mold of clay or wood. The truer splendor lies in the heart. And the real treasure is found when knights or ladies, queens or cowards lay down everything for the King of all hearts.

What does your heart chase after? What treasure do you truly seek—and how far would you go to find it?

ADMIRE

"May the beauty of the LORD our God rest upon us. . ."

Psalm 90:17

JESUS YOU'RE BEAUTIFUL
Nate Sabin

Jesus bright as the morning star
Jesus how can I tell You how beautiful You are to me
Jesus song that the angels sing
Jesus dearer to my heart than anything

Sweeter than springtime
Purer than sunshine
Ever my song will be
Jesus You're beautiful to me

O Lord You are so beautiful
So beautiful so beautiful so beautiful
Jesus You're beautiful to me

If eyes are the windows to a person's soul, it is no wonder that there has never been a rendition of the face of Christ that satisfies my question: What did Jesus look like? What artist could capture the eyes of Immanuel, God with us? What actor could emulate the eyes that act as windows into the very soul of God? We can only make crude and barbaric guesses, and we can only use the poorest substitutes to convey those eyes.

PEOPLE WITHOUT SPIRITUAL
SIGHT MISS BEAUTIFUL
THINGS ALL THE TIME.

And yet, according to Scripture, the Messiah was nothing special to look at. "He had no beauty or majesty to attract us to him, nothing in his appearance that we should desire him" (Isaiah 53:2b). I'm sure many people passed Him on the street or even spoke to Him without pause. People without spiritual sight miss beautiful things all the time, because in kingdom language, what God calls beautiful is not what our world calls beautiful. Though seeing, we do not see (Matthew 13:13). And that is where I find myself.

I am in a world where I am surrounded by unattainable definitions of beauty. I constantly compare myself to airbrushed fiction and question my worth because of my inability to pull off perfection that even the most beautiful people don't really pull off in real life. On a bad day, my favorite thought is that there is another kingdom, and in that other kingdom, beauty has nothing to do with toned thighs and long eyelashes.

But on a *really* bad day, my next thought is, *That's right; it's not about your thighs, it's about your heart,* knowing full well that on a *really* bad day my heart is even more *ugly* than my thighs. Enter Jesus, the Most Beautiful, and " . . . the radiance of

JESUS CAME TO MAKE ME
TRULY BEAUTIFUL
LIKE HE IS TRULY BEAUTIFUL.

God's glory" (Hebrews 1:3). Jesus didn't come to shame me. He didn't come to be perfect and then say, "See, it's easy to be perfect." Jesus came to make me truly beautiful like He is truly beautiful.

Christ took on my appearance when He hung on the cross. The One who had no ugliness in Him became the *ugliest* for me, so that in Him I might become beautiful (2

Corinthians 5:21). Paul says that I can even stand with *confidence* before my Creator: "Through faith in Jesus we may approach God with freedom and confidence" (Ephesians 3:12). I can't imagine standing confidently before a God who sees all things, but because of Christ I can and will stand "without blemish" (Ephesians 5:27).

This is my most humbling thought on a really bad day: *Because Jesus looked like me, I can look like Him. And He is beautiful.*

*In what ways do you recognize
God making you beautiful each day?*

_____

_____

_____

_____

_____

_____

_____

_____

_____

_____

_____

_____

_____

_____

_____

_____

_____

_____

CAPTURE

"If you hear a voice within you say you cannot paint, then by all means paint, and that voice will be silenced."

Vincent Van Gogh

YOU ARE MY KING
Billy James Foote

*I'm forgiven
Because You were forsaken
I'm accepted
You were condemned
I'm alive and well
Your Spirit is within me
Because You died
And rose again*

*Amazing love
How can it be
That You my King
Would die for me
Amazing love
I know it's true
It's my joy to honor You
In all I do I honor You*

*You are my King
Jesus You are my King*

Twenty-Nine

For centuries the Mona Lisa's smile has mystified the poets, the painters, and any passersby who have gazed on the world-renowned portrait. The mystery has always been: Just what was behind that smile that seemed to have a deep, dark secret locked within it?

IT IS THE TRUE SKILL OF ALL
GREAT ARTISTS—TO PORTRAY
WHAT IS OBVIOUS AND TO
HINT AT WHAT IS NOT.

All painters try to capture the seen and the unseen on their canvases, and da Vinci was no exception. What he ended up with, though, did turn out to be exceptional. It is the true skill of all great artists—to portray what is obvious and to hint at what is not. It is the miracle of giving life to something with nothing but paper and paint. Swirled within the combination of light and dark and oil and water and color and space, Leonardo was master enough to make something even more: a splash of art that created a question to leave everyone wondering for centuries. One wonders if he even realized what he was doing.

Albert Einstein, whose mind has been extolled as the ultimate knower of all things, admitted, "The most beautiful thing we can experience is the mysterious." Sometimes knowing the answer, or the story behind, or the explanation for, does little to enhance our appreciation. Sometimes the question is more meaningful than the answer.

Asked to explain how he carved the magnificent

sculpture of David, Michaelangelo simply proclaimed, "I took away everything that wasn't David, until he appeared out of the stone." Yet another mystery for the ages.

> SEPARATING THE DAY FROM
> THE NIGHT WAS THE FIRST
> GREAT ACT OF CREATION—A
> SYMBOL OF WHAT GOD ALSO
> INTENDED TO DO IN OUR LIVES.

All artists, including God, capture truth in stone, in paint, in song, and in life. Separating the day from the night was the first great act of creation—a miracle no artist has yet even dared to explain, a symbol of what He also intended to do in our lives. Unraveling the mystery of it is only half of the canvas, and it's an art only a few brave souls dare attempt.

Everyone looks for tangible love. God left His in every atom ever created. Now we, as artists of life, must find it and show it to the world. Ah, the sweet mystery of life.

Living well is an art. How can you worship God with your daily acts and thoughts? Think of the ways that desire can also transform how you live and relate to others.

_____

_____

_____

_____

_____

_____

_____

_____

_____

_____

_____

_____

_____

_____

_____

_____

_____

_____

_____

WAIT

"Be patient toward all that is unsolved in your heart and try to love the questions themselves. Live the questions now. Perhaps then, someday far in the future, you will gradually, without ever noticing it, live your way into the answer."

Rainer Maria Rilke

I WILL NOT FORGET YOU
Ben Pasley & Robin Pasley

*Many men will drink the rain
And turn to thank the clouds
Many men will hear You speak
They will never turn around*

*But I will not forget
You are my God my King
With a thankful heart
I bring my offering
And my sacrifice is
Not what You can give
But what I alone can
Give to You*

Thirty

No matter how old you get, how many books you read, or how enlightened you become, I am convinced there are three questions you will leave this earth asking without answer: Why, why, and why. I believe that because I don't believe I've ever yet seen anyone leave who had even a close guess. There have been a countless number of theories and theologies and hypotheses attempted, from the sublime to the ridiculous, but nothing that has ever really satisfied the question for anyone who has ever really asked.

I watched a friend lose a child. It was a slow, hope-drenched crawl to a finish no one could believe. I used to think I had at least some of the answers figured out. But as I watched him watch the love of his life slowly fade away and die, I ran out of any possible explanations. I barely can understand when someone has to say good-bye after living many of his years.

What on earth could explain a tiny soul being given time that could be counted in days?

> I BARELY CAN UNDERSTAND
> WHEN SOMEONE HAS TO SAY
> GOOD-BYE AFTER LIVING MANY
> OF HIS YEARS. WHAT ON EARTH
> COULD EXPLAIN A TINY SOUL
> BEING GIVEN TIME THAT COULD
> BE COUNTED IN DAYS?

Elie Wiesel, a Holocaust survivor and writer of stunning memoirs—memoirs of his journey through belief lost and found while in a German concentration camp in World War II—admits the burden of faith in such horrific circumstances: "It seemed as impossible to conceive of Auschwitz with God as to conceive of Aucshwitz without

God. The tragedy of the believer is much greater than the tragedy of the nonbeliever."

> HOLDING ON TO FAITH WHEN
> EVERY SHRED OF EVIDENCE AND
> HAPPENSTANCE POINTS TO
> DESPAIR IS EVEN HARDER THAN
> OUR FIRST LEAPS OF FAITH.

Holding on to faith when every shred of evidence and happenstance points to despair is even harder than our first leaps of faith. It's easy to believe when life is easy. It's easy to let go when life goes wrong. It's easy to doubt when the bombs start to fall.

The world is full of unspeakable, inexplicable horrors.

The less we can explain, the more God's ways escape us. It's mind-numbing to try to reason anything through. I don't know why people have to suffer unimaginably. I don't know why the innocent suffer. I don't even really know why the guilty suffer. I don't know why bad things happen to good people—or why bad things happen at all. There is just no possible explanation.

Flannery O'Connor wrote that it was harder to believe than not to. It is. But I refuse to think it's a game or a test designed by a God bent on seeing His loved ones prove their loyalty through all the outrageous slings and arrows He can throw.

Instead I will wait. And listen. And trust that the answer will be worth every question. And that the bad will transform into something unspeakably good. That every tear will be dried, every wound will be healed. And that one day the Father of all will sit down beside us and explain it once and for all.

What are the "whys" in your life? How have they changed as you've grown in your faith? Which one would you most like to have answered?

_____

_____

_____

_____

_____

_____

_____

_____

_____

_____

_____

_____

_____

_____

_____

_____

_____

_____

MEET WITH ME *by Lamont Hiebert.*
© 1999 Maranatha! Music (admin. by The Copyright Company, Nashville,
TN) c/o The Copyright Company, 1025-16th Avenue South, Suite #204,
Nashville, TN 37212. All rights reserved. Used by permission. CCLI#2753553

ONLY A GOD LIKE YOU *by Tommy Walker.*
© 2000 Integrity's Praise! Music c/o Integrity Media, Inc., 1000 Cody Road,
Mobile, AL 36695. All rights reserved. Used by permission. CCLI#3185395

THE POTTER'S HAND *by Darlene Zschech.*
© 1997 Darlene Zschech/Hillsong Publishing (admin. in the U.S. & Canada
by Integrity's Hosanna! Music) c/o Integrity Media, Inc., 1000 Cody Road,
Mobile, AL 36695. All rights reserved. Used by permission. CCLI#2449771

POWER OF YOUR LOVE *by Geoff Bullock.*
© 1992 Maranatha! Music (admin. by The Copyright Company, Nashville,
TN) and Word Music, Inc. c/o The Copyright Company, 1025-16th Avenue
South, Suite #204, Nashville, TN 37212 and Word Music Group, Inc., 20
Music Square East, Nashville, TN 37203. All rights reserved. Used by permis-
sion. CCLI#917491

RISE UP AND PRAISE HIM *by Paul Baloche and Gary Sadler.*
© 1996 Integrity's Hosanna! Music c/o Integrity Media, Inc., 1000 Cody
Road, Mobile, AL 36695. All rights reserved. Used by permission.
CCLI#2060552

ROCK OF AGES *by Rita Baloche.*
© 1997 Maranatha Praise, Inc. (admin. by The Copyright Company, Nashville,
TN) c/o The Copyright Company, 1025-16th Avenue South, Suite #204,
Nashville, TN 37212. All rights reserved. Used by permission. CCLI#1189479

SHOUT TO THE NORTH *by Martin Smith.*
© 1995 Curious? Music UK (All rights admin. in the U.S. & Canada by EMI
Christian Music Publishing) c/o EMI Christian Music Publishing, Inc., PO
Box 5085, 101 Winners Circle, Brentwood, TN 37024. All rights reserved.
Used by permission. CCLI#1562261